THOUGHTS,

SELECTED FROM THE WRITINGS

OF THE

REV. WILLIAM E. CHANNING, D. D.

BY HENRY A. MILES.

"Sometimes a single word, spoken by the voice of genius, goes far into the heart. A hint, a suggestion, an undefined delicacy of expression, teaches more than we gather from volumes of less gifted men." — *Channing.*

ELEVENTH THOUSAND.

BOSTON:
WALKER, WISE, AND COMPANY,
PUBLISHERS FOR THE
AMERICAN UNITARIAN ASSOCIATION,
21 Bromfield St.
1859.

PREFACE.

THE following pages are made up entirely of short sentences selected from the writings of Dr. Channing. There is probably no other author of the age from whose works a greater number of striking detached thoughts may be gathered. The fact is attributable not only, nor chiefly, to the wide range of subjects to which he turned his attention — Theology, Morals, Literature, Politics, Education, Social Life, Reforms — but, still more, to the *aphoristic* style of expression in which it is evident that he both delighted and excelled. Thus, all who heard his preaching, or have read his works, will remember how frequently some great truth, to the unfolding of which perhaps several pages were devoted, was at last summed up and condensed, in a single, brief, beautiful, and memorable sentence; and many of these "apples of gold in pictures of silver" are brought together in this little book. No doubt the reader will miss favorite passages, and yet it is not doubted, also, that he will recognize in the following pages many of those pointed sayings and deep thoughts with which he has felt it to be good to commune. In this miniature form they can be carried about one's person, in the steamboat and car, and when seeking health or recreation by the seashore or the mountain side. The little volume is intended, also, as a choice gift to a friend; and, perchance, it may introduce some to an acquaintance with this great Benefactor to our minds, who, through sectarian fears, might be repelled from a larger work. Thus, these seeds of great thoughts may be scattered even by little wings, just as the seeds of the greatest trees of the forest are scattered by the smallest bird.

H. A. M.

THOUGHTS.

An humble spire, pointing heavenward from an obscure church, speaks of man's nature, man's dignity, man's destiny, more eloquently than all the columns and arches of Greece and Rome, the mausoleums of Asia, or the pyramids of Egypt.

One great and kindling thought from a retired and obscure man, may live when thrones are fallen, and the memory of those who filled them obliterated, and, like an undying fire, may illuminate and quicken all future generations.

The worst error in religion, after all, is that of the skeptic, who records triumphantly the weaknesses and wanderings of the human intellect, and maintains that no trust is due to the decisions of this erring reason. We by no means conceive that man's greatest danger springs from pride of understanding, though we think as badly of this vice as other Christians. The history of the church proves that men may trust their faculties too little as well as too much, and that the timidity, which shrinks from investigation, has injured the mind, and betrayed the interests of Christianity, as much as an irreverent boldness of thought.

It is one sign of the tendency of human nature to goodness, that it grows good under a thousand bad influences.

No books astonish me like the Gospels. Jesus, the hero of the story, is a more extraordinary being than imagination has feigned, and yet his character has an impress of nature, consistency, truth, never surpassed. You have all seen portraits, which, as soon as seen, you felt to be likenesses, so living were they, so natural, so true. Such is the impression made on my mind by the Gospels. I believe that you or I could lift mountains or create a world as easily as fanaticism or imposture could have created such a character and history as that of Jesus Christ.

God be thanked for books! They are the voices of the distant and the dead, and make us heirs of the spiritual life of past ages. Books are the true levellers. They give to all, who will faithfully use them, the society, the spiritual presence, of the best and greatest of our race. No matter how poor I am. No matter though the prosperous of my own time will not enter my obscure dwelling. If the sacred writers will enter and take up their abode under my roof, if Milton will cross my threshold to sing to me of Paradise, or Shakspeare to open to me the worlds of imagination and the workings of the human heart, and Franklin to enrich me with his practical wisdom, I shall not pine for want of intellectual companionship; and I may become a cultivated man, though excluded from what is called the best society in the place where I live.

It is common to speak of the house of public worship as a holy place; but it has no exclusive sanctity. The holiest spot on earth, is that where the soul breathes its purest vows, and forms or executes its noblest purposes; and on this ground, were I to seek the holiest spot in your city, I should not go to your splendid sanctuaries, but to closets of private prayer. Perhaps the "Holy of Holies" among you is some dark, narrow room, from which most of us would shrink as unfit for human habitation; but God dwells there. He hears there music more grateful than the swell of all your organs; sees there a beauty such as nature, in her robes of Spring, does not unfold; for there he meets, and sees, and hears, the humblest, most thankful, most trustful worshipper; sees the sorest trials serenely borne, the deepest injuries forgiven; sees toils and sacrifices cheerfully sustained, and death approached, through a lonely illness, with a triumphant faith. The consecration which such virtues shed over the obscurest spot is not and cannot be communicated by any of those outward rites by which our splendid structures are dedicated to God.

ONE great principle, which we should lay down as immovably true, is, that if a good work cannot be carried on by the calm, self-controlled, benevolent spirit of Christianity, then the time for doing it has not come. God asks not the aid of our vices. He can overrule them for good, but they are not the chosen instruments of human happiness.

No department of literature is so false as biography. The object is, not to let down the hero; and consequently what is most human, most genuine, most characteristic in his history is excluded. Sometimes, one anecdote will let us into the secret of a man's soul, more than all the prominent events of his life.

You know that on earth we sometimes meet human beings, whose countenances, at the first view, scatter all distrust, and win from us something like the reliance of a long-tried friendship.

One smile is enough to let us into their hearts, to reveal to us a goodness on which we may repose. That smile with which Jesus will meet the new-born inhabitant of heaven, that joyful greeting, that beaming of love from him who bled for us, that tone of welcome — all these I can faintly conceive, but no language can utter them. The joys of centuries will be crowded into that meeting. This is not fiction. It is truth, founded on the essential laws of the mind.

The greatest benefactor to society is not he who serves it by single acts, but whose general character is the manifestation of a higher life and spirit than pervades the mass.

How deeply do I commiserate the minister, who, in the warmth and freshness of youth, is visited with glimpses of higher truth than is imbodied in the creed, but who dares not be just to himself, and is made to echo what is not the simple, natural expression of his own mind!

—♦—

WHEN we think that every house might be cheered by intelligence, disinterestedness, and refinement, and then remember in how many houses the higher powers and affections of human nature are buried as in tombs, what a darkness gathers over society!

—♦—

FASHION is a poor vocation. Its creed, that idleness is a privilege and work a disgrace, is among the deadliest errors. Without depth of thought, or earnestness of feeling, or strength of purpose, living an unreal life, sacrificing substance to show, substituting the fictitious for the natural, mistaking a crowd for society, finding its chief pleasure in ridicule, and exhausting its ingenuity in expedients for killing time, fashion is among the last influences under which a human being, who respects himself, or who comprehends the great end of life, would desire to be placed.

TRUE religion is a life unfolded within, not something forced on us from abroad.

THE father and mother of an unnoticed family, who, in their seclusion, awaken the mind of one child to the idea and love of perfect goodness, who awaken in him a strength of will to repel all temptation, and who send him out prepared to profit by the conflicts of life, surpass in influence a Napoleon, breaking the world to his sway. And not only is their work higher in kind; who knows but that they are doing a greater work, even as to extent and surface, than the conqueror? Who knows, but that the being, whom they inspire with holy and disinterested principles, may communicate himself to others; and that, by a spreading agency, of which they were the silent origin, improvements may spread through a nation, through the world?

No doctrine is more common among Christians than that of man's immortality; but it is not so generally understood, that the germs or principles of his whole future being are now wrapped up in his soul, as the rudiments of the future plant in the seed. As a necessary result of this constitution, the soul, possessed and moved by these mighty though infant energies, is perpetually stretching beyond what is present and visible, struggling against the bounds of its earthly prison-house, and seeking relief and joy in imaginings of unseen and ideal being. This view of our nature, which has never been fully developed, and which goes further towards explaining the contradictions of human life than all others, carries us to the very foundations and sources of poetry. He who cannot interpret by his own consciousness what we now have said, wants the true key to the works of genius. He has not penetrated those secret recesses of the soul, where Poetry is born and nourished, and inhales immortal vigor, and wings herself for her heavenward flight.

A POOR man, living on bread and water, because he will not ask for more than bare sustenance requires, and leading a quiet, cheerful life through his benevolent sympathies, his joy in duty, his trust in God, is one of the true heroes of the race, and understands better the meaning of happiness than we, who cannot be at ease unless we clothe ourselves "in purple, and fare sumptuously every day;" unless we surround, defend, and adorn ourselves, with all the products of nature and art. His scantiness of outward means is a sign of inward fulness; whilst the slavery, in which most of us live, to luxuries and accommodations, shows the poverty within.

Religion, as it has been generally taught, is any thing but an elevating principle. It has been used to scare the child, and appal the adult. Men have been virtually taught to glorify God by flattery, rather than by becoming excellent and glorious themselves, and thus doing honor to their Maker. Our dependence on God has been so taught, as to extinguish the consciousness of our free nature and moral power. Religion, in one or another form, has always been an engine for crushing the human soul. But such is not the religion of Jesus Christ. If it were, it would deserve no respect.

The surest device for making the mind a coward and a slave, is a wide-spread and closely-cemented church, the powers of which are concentrated in the hands of a "sacred order," and which has succeeded in arrogating to its rites or ministers a sway over the future world, over the soul's everlasting weal or woe. The inevitably degrading influence of such a church is demonstrative proof against its divine original.

The abolition of war is no longer to be set down as a creation of fancy, a dream of enthusiastic philanthropy War rests on opinion; and opinion is more and more withdrawing its support. War rests on contempt of human nature; on the long mournful habit of regarding the mass of human beings as machines, or as animals; having no higher use than to be shot at and murdered for the glory of a chief, for the seating of this or that family on a throne, for the petty interests and selfish rivalries which have inflamed states to conflict. Let the worth of a human being be felt, and a main pillar of war will fall.

A SECT which has true life will seize by instinct the emblems and rites which are in accordance with itself; and without life, it will only find in borrowed rites its winding-sheet.

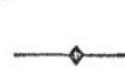

IT has been the fault of all sects, that they have been too anxious to define their religion. They have labored to circumscribe the infinite. Christianity, as it exists in the mind of the true disciple, is not made up of fragments, of separate ideas, which he can express in detached propositions. It is a vast and ever-unfolding whole, pervaded by one spirit; each precept and doctrine deriving its vitality from its union with all. When I see this generous, heavenly doctrine compressed and cramped in human creeds, I feel as I should were I to see screws and chains applied to the countenance and limbs of a noble fellow-creature, deforming and destroying one of the most beautiful works of God.

INFLUENCE is to be measured, not by the extent of surface it covers, but by its *kind*. A man may spread his mind, his feelings, and opinions, through a great extent, but, if his mind be a low one, he manifests no greatness. A wretched artist may fill a city with daubs, and, by a false, showy style, achieve a reputation; but the man of genius, who leaves behind him one grand picture, in which immortal beauty is imbodied, and which is silently to spread a true taste in his art, exerts an incomparably higher influence.

THE best style is not that which puts the reader most easily and in the shortest time in possession of a writer's naked thoughts, but that which is the truest image of a great intellect, which conveys fully, and carries farthest into other souls, the conceptions and feelings of a profound and lofty spirit.

A BLOW given to a single slave is a stripe on the souls of all who see or hear it. It makes all abject, servile. It is not the wound given to the flesh of which we now complain. Scar the back, and you have done nothing, compared with the wrong done to the soul.

You have either stung that soul with infernal passions, with thirst for revenge, or, what perhaps is more discouraging, you have broken and brutalized it. The human spirit has perished under your hands, as far as it can be destroyed by human force.

We have all felt, when looking above us into the atmosphere, that there was an infinity of space which we could not explore. When I look into man's spirit, and see there the germs of an immortal life, I feel more deeply that an infinity lies hid beyond what I see. In the idea of duty, which springs up in every human heart, I discern a law more sacred and boundless than gravitation, which binds the soul to a more glorious universe than that to which attraction binds the body, and which is to endure though the laws of physical nature pass away. Every moral sentiment, every intellectual action, is to me a hint, a prophetic sign, of a spiritual power to be expanded forever; just as a faint ray from a distant star is significant of unimaginable splendor.

Most Protestant sects are built on the Papal foundation. Their creeds and excommunications imbody the grand idea of infallibility, as truly as the decrees of Trent and the Vatican.

If they who wear the chains of creeds once knew the happiness of breathing the air of freedom, and of moving with an unencumbered spirit, no wealth or power in the world's gift would bribe them to part with their spiritual liberty.

Our Christian principles must work a new miracle, must exercise and expel the spirit of caste. The strength, happiness, and true civilization of a community are determined by nothing more than by a fraternal union among all conditions of men. Without this, a civil war virtually rages in a state.

A THEOLOGY at war with the laws of physical nature, would be a battle of no doubtful issue. The laws of our spiritual nature give still less chance of success to the system which would thwart or stay them.

WE never know a great character until something congenial to it has grown up within ourselves.

I AM not sorry that society is taxed for the drunkard. I would it were taxed more. I would the burden of sustaining him were so heavy, that we should be compelled to wake up, and ask how he may be saved from ruin.

THE dissensions of Protestantism go far to constitute its strength. Through them its spirit, which is freedom, the only spirit which Rome cannot conquer, is kept alive.

WE do not find that civilization lightens men's toils: as yet it has increased them; and in this I see the sign of a deep defect in what we call the progress of society.

MIRACLES, when considered in a general, abstract manner, — that is, when divested of all circumstances, and supposed to occur as disconnected facts, to stand alone in history, to have no explanations or reasons in preceding events, and no influence on those which follow, — are indeed open to great objection, as wanton and useless violations of nature's order; and it is accordingly against miracles, considered in this naked, general form, that the arguments of infidelity are chiefly urged. But it is great disingenuity to class under this head the miracles of Christianity. They are palpably different. They do not stand alone in history, but are most intimately incorporated with it. They were demanded by the state of the world which preceded them, and they have left deep traces on all subsequent ages. In fact, the history of the whole civilized world, since their alleged occurrence, has been swayed and colored by them, and is wholly inexplicable without them.

To me the progress of society consists in nothing more than in bringing out the individual, in giving him a consciousness of his own being, and in quickening him to strengthen and elevate his own mind.

THERE are authors in approaching whom we are conscious of an access of intellectual strength. A "virtue goes out" from them. Sometimes a single word, spoken by the voice of genius, goes far into the heart. A hint, a suggestion, an undefined delicacy of expression, teaches more than we gather from volumes of less gifted men. The works which we should chiefly study are not those which contain the greatest fund of knowledge, but which raise us into sympathy with the intellectual energy of the author, and through which a great mind multiplies itself, as it were, in the reader.

To a man who cherishes a sense of God, the great difficulty is, not to account for miracles, but to account for their rare occurrence. One of the mysteries of the universe is this — that its Author retires so continually behind the veil of his works; that the great and good Father does not manifest himself more distinctly to his creatures. There is something like coldness and repulsiveness in instructing us only by fixed, inflexible laws of nature. The intercourse of God with Adam and the patriarchs suits our best conceptions of the relation which he bears to the human race, and ought not to surprise us more than the expressions of a human parent's tenderness and concern towards his offspring.

NATURE is no Trinitarian. It gives not a hint, not a glimpse, of a tripersonal author. Trinitarianism is a confined system, shut up in a few texts, a few written lines, where many of the wisest minds have failed to discover it. It is not inscribed on the heavens and the earth, not borne on every wind, not resounding and reëchoing through the universe. The sun and stars say nothing of a God of three persons. They all speak of the One Father whom we adore. To our ears one and the same voice comes from God's word and works, a full and swelling strain, growing clearer, louder, more thrilling as we listen, and with one blessed influence lifting up our souls to the Almighty Father.

I FEAR the spirit of science, at the present day, is too often a degradation rather than the true culture of the soul. It is the bowing down of the heaven-born spirit before unthinking mechanism. It seeks knowledge rather for animal, transitory purposes, than for the nutriment of the imperishable inward life; and yet the worshippers of science pity or contemn the poor, because denied this means of cultivation. Unhappy poor! Shut out from libraries, laboratories, and learned institutes! In view of this world's wisdom, it avails you nothing that your own nature, manifested in your own and other souls, that God's word and works, that the ocean, earth, and sky, are laid open to you; that you may acquaint yourselves with the divine perfections, with the character of Christ, with the duties of life, with the virtues, the generous sacrifices, and the beautiful and holy emotions, which are a revelation and pledge of heaven. All these are nothing, do not lift you to the rank of cultivated men, because the mysteries of the telescope and microscope, of the air-pump and crucible, are not revealed to you! I would they were revealed to you. I believe the time is coming when Christian benevolence will delight in spreading all truth and all refinements through all ranks of society But meanwhile be not discouraged. One ray of moral and religious truth is worth all the wisdom of the schools. One lesson from

Christ will carry you higher than years of study under those who are too enlightened to follow this celestial guide.

We wonder, indeed, when we are told, that one day we shall be as the angels of God. I apprehend that as great a wonder has been realized already on the earth. I apprehend that the distance between the mind of Newton and of a Hottentot may have been as great as between Newton and an angel. There is another view still more striking. This Newton, who lifted his calm, sublime eye to the heavens, and read among the planets and the stars the great law of the material universe, was, forty or fifty years before, an infant, without one clear perception, and unable to distinguish his nurse's arm from the pillow on which he slept. Howard, too, who, under the strength of an all-sacrificing benevolence, explored the depths of human suffering, was, forty or fifty years before, an infant, wholly absorbed in himself, grasping at all he saw, and almost breaking his little heart with fits of passion, when the idlest toy was withheld. Has not man already traversed as wide a space as separates him from angels?

One of the excellences of Christianity is, that it is not an abstruse theory, not wrapped up in abstract phrases, but taught us in facts, in narratives. It lives, moves, speaks, and acts before our eyes. Christian love is not taught us in cold precepts. It speaks from the cross. So immortality is not a vague promise. It breaks forth like the morning from the tomb near Calvary. It becomes a glorious reality in the person of the rising Savior, and his ascension opens to our view the heaven into which he enters. It is this historical form of our religion which peculiarly adapts it to childhood, to the imagination and heart which open first in childhood.

THE church is important only as it ministers to purity of heart and life; and every church which so ministers is a good one; no matter how, when, or where it grew up; no matter whether it worship on its knees, or on its feet, or whether its ministers are ordained by pope, bishop, presbyter, or people; these are secondary things, and of no comparative moment. The church which opens on heaven is that, and that only, in which the spirit of heaven dwells. The church where worship rises to God's ear is that, and that only, where the soul ascends. No matter whether it be gathered in cathedral or barn; whether it sit in silence or send up a hymn; whether the minister speak from carefully-prepared notes, or from immediate, fervent, irrepressible suggestion. If God be loved, and Jesus Christ be welcomed to the soul, and his instructions be meekly and wisely heard, and the solemn purpose grow up to do all duty amidst all conflict, sacrifice, and temptation, then the true end of the church is answered. "This is no other than the house of God, the gate of heaven.'

Free trade! — this is the plain duty and the plain interest of the human race. To level all barriers to free exchange, to cut up the system of restriction, root and branch, to open every port on earth to every product, — this is the office of enlightened humanity. To this a free nation should especially pledge itself. Freedom of the seas, freedom of harbors, an intercourse of nations free as the winds, — this is not a dream of philanthropists. We are tending towards it, and let us hasten it. Under a wiser and more Christian civilization we shall look back on our present restrictions as we do on the swaddling bands by which, in darker times, the human body was compressed.

I do not think that so much harm is done by giving error to a child, as by giving truth in a lifeless form.

It is by his personal endowments, by his intellectual, moral, and religious worth, by his faithfulness and zeal, and not through any mysterious ceremony or power, that the minister enlightens and edifies the church. What matters it how he is ordained and set apart, if he give himself to his work in the fear of God? What matters it who has laid hands on him, or whether he stands up in surplice or drab coat? I go to church to be benefited, not by hands or coats, but by the action of an enlightened and holy teacher on my mind and heart; not an overpowering, irresistible action, but such as becomes effectual through my own free thought and will. I go to be convinced of what is true, and to be warmed with love of what is good; and he who thus helps me is a true minister, no matter from what school, consistory, or ecclesiastical body, he comes. He carries his commission in his soul. Do not say that his ministry has no "validity," because Rome, or Geneva, or Lambeth, or Andover, or Princeton, has not laid hands on him. What! has he not opened my eyes to see, and roused my conscience to reprove? As I have heard him, has not my heart burned within me, and have I not silently given myself to God with new humility and love? Has he not taught and helped me to deny myself, to conquer the world, to do good to a foe? Have I not been pierced by his warnings, and softened by his looks and tones of love? Has he done this, and yet has his ministry no "validity"? What other validity can there be than this? If a generous friend gives me water to drink when I am parched with thirst, and I drink and am refreshed, will it do to tell me that because he did not buy the cup at a certain licensed shop, or draw the water at a certain antiquated cistern, therefore his act of kindness is "invalid," and I am as thirsty and weak as I was before? What more can a minister with mitre or tiara do than help me, by wise and touching manifestations of God's truth, to become a holier, nobler man? If my soul be made alive, no matter who ministers to me; and if not, the ordinances of the church, whether high or low, orthodox or heretical, are of no validity, so far as I am concerned. The diseased man who is restored to health cares little whether his physician wears wig or cowl, or receives his diploma from Paris or London; and so to the regenerate man it is of little moment where, or by what processes, he became a temple of the Holy Spirit.

MEN, in general, cannot now endure to think that their own narrow church holds all the goodness on the earth. True, much intolerance remains; its separating walls are not fallen; but, with a few exceptions, they no longer reach to the clouds. Many of them have crumbled away, till the men whom they sever can shake hands, and exchange words of fellowship, and recognize in one another's faces the features of brethren.

THE day-laborer, who earns, with horny hand and the sweat of his face, coarse food for a wife and children whom he loves, is raised, by this generous motive, to true dignity; and, though wanting the refinements of life, is a nobl[illegible] being than those who think themselves absolved by wealth from serving others.

The great sources of intellectual power and progress to a people are its strong and original thinkers, be they found where they may. Government cannot, and does not, extend the bounds of knowledge; cannot make experiments in the laboratory, explore the laws of animal or vegetable nature, or establish the principles of criticism, morals, and religion. The energy which is to carry forward the intellect of a people, belongs chiefly to private individuals, who devote themselves to lonely thought, who worship truth, who originate the views demanded by their age, who help us to throw off the yoke of established prejudices, who improve old modes of education or invent better. It is true that great men at the head of affairs may, and often do, contribute much to the growth of a nation's mind. But it too often happens that their station obstructs, rather than aids, their usefulness. Their connection with a party, and the habit of viewing subjects in reference to personal aggrandizement, too often obscure the noblest intellects, and convert into patrons of narrow views and temporary interests those who, in other conditions, would have been the lights of their age, and the propagators of everlasting truth.

Men who, to support a creed, would shake our trust in the calm, deliberate, and distinct decisions of our rational and moral powers, endanger religion more than its open foes, and forge the deadliest weapon for the infidel.

All Protestant sects tell the learner to listen to Jesus Christ; but most of them shout around him their own articles so vehemently and imperiously, that the voice of the heavenly Master is well nigh drowned. He is told to listen to Christ, but told that he will be damned if he receives any lessons but such as are taught in the creed. He is told that Christ's word alone is infallible, but that, unless it is received as interpreted by fallible men, he will be excluded from the communion of Christians. This is what shocks me in the creed-maker. He interposes himself between me and my Savior. He dares not trust me alone with Jesus. He dares not leave me the word of God.

No punishment is so terrible as prosperous guilt.

Do not, as some do, look on the child as born under the curse of God; as naturally hostile to all goodness and truth. What! the child totally depraved! Can it be that such a thought ever entered the mind of a human being? especially of a parent! What! in the beauty of childhood and youth, in that open brow, that cheerful smile, do you see the brand of total corruption? Is it a little fiend who sleeps so sweetly on his mother's breast? Was it an infant demon, which Jesus took in his arms, and said, "Of such is the kingdom of heaven"? Is the child, who, as you relate to him a story of suffering or generosity, listens with a tearful or kindling eye and a throbbing heart, is *he* a child of hell? As soon could I look on the sun, and think it the source of darkness, as on the countenance of childhood and youth, and see total depravity written there.

Public opinion cannot do for virtue what it does for vice. It is the essence of virtue to look above opinion. Vice is consistent with, and very often strengthened by, entire subserviency to it.

HE that can understand and delight in greatness was created to partake of it; the germ is in him; and sometimes this admiration, in what we deem inferior minds, discovers a nobler spirit than belongs to the great man who awakens it; for sometimes the great man is so absorbed in his own greatness, as to admire no other; and I should not hesitate to say, that a common mind, which is yet capable of a generous admiration, is destined to rise higher than the man of eminent capacities, who can enjoy no power or excellence but his own.

THAT piety may exist, it is not enough to know that God alone, and constantly, sustains all beings. This is not a foundation for moral feeling towards him. The great question on which religion rests, is, *What kind* of a universe does he create and sustain? Were a being of vast power to give birth to a system of unmeasured, unmitigated evil, dependence on him would be any thing but a ground of reverence. We should hate it, and long to flee from it into non-existence. The great question, I repeat, is, What is the nature, the end, the purpose of the creation which God upholds? On this, and on the relations growing out of this, religion wholly rests.

Did I believe, what Trinitarianism teaches, that not the least transgression, not even the first sin of the dawning mind of the child, can be remitted without an infinite expiation, I should feel myself living under a legislation unspeakably dreadful, under laws written, like Draco's, in blood; and, instead of thanking the Sovereign for providing an infinite substitute, I should shudder at the attributes which render this expedient necessary.

BETTER be cold than affect to feel. In truth, nothing is so cold as an assumed, noisy enthusiasm. Its best emblem is the northern blast of winter, which freezes as it roars.

To myself the most effectual church is that in which I see the signs of Christian affection in those around me, in which warm hearts are beating on every side, in which a deep stillness speaks of the absorbed soul, in which I recognize fellow-beings, who, in common life, have impressed me with their piety. One look from a beaming countenance, one tone in singing from a deeply-moved heart, perhaps aids me more than the sermon. When nothing is said, I feel it to be good to be among the devout; and I wonder not that the Quakers, in some of their still meetings, profess to hold the most intimate union, not only with God, but with each other. It is not with the voice only that man communicates with man. Nothing is so eloquent as the deep silence of a crowd. A sigh, a low breathing, sometimes pours into us our neighbor's soul more than a volume of words. There is a communication more subtile than freemasonry between those who feel alike. How contagious is holy feeling! On the other hand, how freezing, how palsying is the gathering of a multitude who feel nothing, who come to God's house without reverence, without love, who gaze around on each other as if they were assembled at a show, whose restlessness keeps up a slightly-disturbing sound, whose countenances reveal no collectedness, no earnestness, but a frivolous or absent mind! The very sanctity of the place makes this indifference more chilling. One of the coldest spots on earth is a church without devotion. What is it to me that a costly temple is set apart, by ever so many rites, for God's service, that priests, who trace their lineage to the apostles, have consecrated it, if I find it thronged by the worldly and undevout? This is no church to me. I go to meet, not human bodies, but souls; and if I find them in an upper room, like that where the first disciples met, or in a shed, or in a street, there I find a church; there is the true altar, the sweet incense, the accepted priest. These all I find in sanctified souls.

GREAT nations, like great boys, place their honor in resisting insult, and in fighting well. One would think the time had gone by, in which nations needed to rush to arms, to prove that they were not cowards. If there is one truth which history has taught, it is that communities, in all stages of society, from the most barbarous to the most civilized, have sufficient courage. No people can charge upon its conscience that it has not shed blood enough in proof of its valor. Almost any man, under the usual stimulants of the camp, can stand fire.

To leave a people to themselves, is generally the best service their rulers can render.

STATESMEN work in the dark, until the idea of right towers above expediency or wealth.

THE human being has been subjected to a stern criticism. It has been forgotten that he is as yet an infant, new to existence, unconscious of his powers; and he has been expected to see clearly, walk firmly, and act perfectly. Especially in estimating his transgressions, the chief regard has been had, not to his finite nature and present stage of development, but to the infinity of the being against whom he has sinned; so that God's greatness, instead of being made a ground of hope, has been used to plunge man into despair.

It is said that, in forming civil society, the individual surrenders a part of his rights. It would be more proper to say that he adopts new modes of securing them.

By looking at the sun, we lose the power of seeing other objects. It was, I conceive, one design of God, in hiding himself so far from us, in throwing around himself the veil of his works, to prevent this very evil. He intended that our faculties should be left at liberty to act on other things beside himself; that the will should not be crushed by his overpowering greatness; that we should be free agents; that we should recognize rights in ourselves and in others, as well as in the Creator, and thus be introduced into a wide and ever-enlarging sphere of action and duty.

Men's characters are determined, not by the opinions which they profess, but by those on which their thoughts habitually fasten, which recur to them most forcibly, and which color their ordinary views of God and duty. The creed of habit, imitation, or fear, may be defended stoutly, and yet have little practical influence. The mind, when compelled, by education or other circumstances, to receive irrational doctrines, has yet a power of keeping them, as it were, on its surface, of excluding them from its depths, of refusing to incorporate them with its own being; and when burdened with a mixed and incongruous system, it often discovers a sagacity which reminds us of the instinct of inferior animals, in selecting the healthful and nutritious portions, and in making *them* its daily food. Accordingly, the real faith often corresponds little with that which is professed. It often happens, that, through the progress of the mind in light and virtue, opinions, once central, are gradually thrown outward, lose their vitality, and cease to be principles of action, whilst through habit they are defended as articles of faith.

SOCIAL order is better preserved by liberty than by restraint. A community which should open a great variety of spheres to its members, so that all might find free scope for their powers, would need little array of force for restraint. Liberty would prove the best peace-officer. The social order of New England, without a soldier, and almost without a police, bears loud witness to this truth.

We hear much at present of efforts to spread the gospel. But Christianity is gaining more by the removal of degrading errors, than it would by armies of missionaries who should carry with them a corrupted form of the religion.

It is the sensualities, the earthliness, of those who give the tone to public sentiment, which is chargeable with a vast amount of the intemperance of the poor.

Suppose that we meet together in a place consecrated by all manner of forms, but that nothing of Christ's spirit dwells in us. With all its forms, it is a synagogue of Satan, not a church of Jesus. Christ in the hearts of men is the only church bond. The Catholics, to give them a feeling of the present Savior, adorn their temples with paintings, representing him in the most affecting scenes of his life and death; and had worship never been directed to these, I should not object to them. But there is a far higher likeness to Christ than the artist ever drew or chiseled. It exists in the heart of his true disciple. The true disciple surpasses Raphael and Michael Angelo.

It is strange that laboring men do not think more of the vast usefulness of their toils, and take a benevolent pleasure in them on this account. One would think that a carpenter or mason, on passing a house which he had reared, would say to himself, "This work of mine is giving comfort and enjoyment every day and every hour to a family, and will continue to be a kindly shelter, a domestic gathering-place, an abode of affection, for a century or more after I sleep in the dust;" and ought not a generous satisfaction to spring up at the thought?

There is no portion of human history more humbling than that of sects. When I meditate on the grand moral, spiritual purpose of Christianity, in which all its glory consists; when I consider how plainly Christianity attaches importance to nothing but to the moral excellence, the disinterested, divine virtue, which was imbodied in the teaching and life of its founder; and when, from this position, I look down on the sects which have figured, and now figure, in the church; when I see them making such a stir about matters generally so unessential; when I see them seizing on a disputed and disputable doctrine, making it a watchword, a test of God's favor, a bond of communion, a ground of self-complacency, a badge of peculiar holiness, a warrant for condemning its rejectors, however imbued with the spirit of Christ; when I see them overlooking the weightier matters of the law, and laying infinite stress here on a bishop and prayer-book, there on the quantity of water applied in baptism, and there on some dark solution of an incomprehensible article of faith; when I see the mock dignity of their exclusive claims to truth, to churchship, to the promises of God's word; when I hear the mimic thunderbolts of denunciation and excommunication which they delight to hurl; when I consider how their deep theology, in proportion as it is examined, evaporates into words, how many opposite and extravagant notions are covered by the same broad shield of mystery and tradition, and how commonly the persuasion of infallibility is proportioned to the absurdity of the creed; when I consider these things, and other matters of like import, I am lost in amazement at the amount of arrogant folly, of self-complacent intolerance, of almost incredible blindness to the end and essence of Christianity, which the history of sects reveals.

I SEE in Christianity nothing narrowing or depressing, nothing of the littleness of the systems which human craft, fear, and ambition have engendered. I meet there no minute legislation, no descending to precise details, no arbitrary injunctions, no yoke of ceremonies, no outward religion. Every thing breathes freedom, liberality, enlargement. I meet there, not a formal, rigid creed, binding on the intellect, through all ages, the mechanical, passive repetition of the same words and the same ideas; but I meet a few grand, all-comprehending truths, which are given to the soul to be developed and applied by itself; given to it, as seed to the sower, to be cherished and expanded by its own thought, love, and obedience, into more and more glorious fruits of wisdom and virtue.

WITH few exceptions, the Trinitarian theology of the present day is greatly deficient in freshness of thought, and in power to awaken the interest, and to meet the intellectual and spiritual wants, of thinking men. I see, indeed, superior minds, and great minds among the adherents of the prevalent system, but they seem to me to move in chains, and to fulfil poorly their high functions of adding to the wealth of the human intellect. In theological discussion, they remind me more of Samson grinding in the narrow mill of the Philistines, than of that undaunted champion achieving victories for God's people, and enlarging the bounds of their inheritance.

In discussions of an irritating nature, the true way of doing good is, to purify ourselves from all unworthy motives, to cherish disinterested sentiments and unaffected good-will towards those from whom we differ, and then to leave the mind to utter itself naturally and spontaneously. Nothing is to be gained by caution, circumlocution, plausible softenings of language, and other arts, which, in destroying confidence, defeat their own end.

The passion for gain is every where sapping pure and generous feeling, and every where raises up bitter foes against any reform which may threaten to turn aside a stream of wealth. I sometimes feel as if a great social revolution were necessary to break up our present mercenary civilization, in order that Christianity, now repelled by the almost universal worldliness, may come into new contact with the soul, and may reconstruct society after its own pure and disinterested principles.

Trinitarianism is a riddle. Men call it a mystery; but it is mysterious, not like the great truths of religion, by its vastness and grandeur, but by the irreconcilable ideas which it involves.

Monks shut up in cells; a priesthood cut off by celibacy from the sympathies and most interesting relations in life; and universities enslaved to a scholastic logic, and taught to place wisdom in verbal subtilties and unintelligible definitions, — these took Christianity into their keeping; and, at their chilling touch, this generous religion, so full of life and affection, became a dry, frigid, abstract system. Christianity, as it came from their hands, and as it has been transmitted by a majority of Protestant divines, reminds us of the human form, compressed by swathing-bands, until every joint is rigid, every movement constrained, and almost all the beauty and grace of nature obliterated.

To one who reflects, there is something very shocking in the decorations of war. If men must fight, let them wear the badges which become their craft. It would shock us to see a hangman dressed out in scarf and epaulet, and marching with merry music to the place of punishment. The soldier has a sadder work than the hangman. His office is not to despatch occasionally a single criminal; he goes to the slaughter of thousands as free from crime as himself. The sword is worn as an ornament; and yet its use is to pierce the heart of a fellow-creature. As well might the butcher parade before us his knife, or the executioner his axe or halter. Allow war to be necessary, — still it is a horrible necessity, a work to fill a good man with anguish of spirit. Shall it be turned into an occasion of pomp and merriment?

Woe to that church which looks round for forms to wake it up to spiritual life. The dying man is not to be revived by a new dress, however graceful.

The dress of Europe, not many centuries ago, was fashioned very much after what may be called the harlequin style; that is, it affected strong colors and strong contrasts. This taste belongs to rude ages, and has passed away very much with the progress of civilization. The military dress alone has escaped the reform. The military man is the only harlequin left us from ancient times.

The creed-maker defines Jesus in half a dozen lines, perhaps in metaphysical terms, and calls me to assent to this account of my Savior. I learn less of Christ by this process than I should learn of the sun, by being told that this glorious luminary is a circle about a foot in diameter.

The most effectual method of expelling error, is, not to meet it sword in hand, but gradually to instil great truths, with which it cannot easily coëxist, and by which the mind outgrows it. The old superstitions about ghosts and dreams were not expelled by argument, — for hardly a book was written against them;

but men gradually outgrew them; and the spectres which had haunted the terror-stricken soul for ages, fled before an improved philosophy, just as they were supposed to vanish before the rising sun.

He who does a bad deed says, more strongly than words can utter, "I cast away a portion of future good; I resolve on future pain."

One and only one evil can be carried from this world to the next, and that is, the evil within us, moral evil, — guilt, crime, ungoverned passion, the depraved mind, the memory of a wasted or ill-spent life, the character which has grown up under neglect of God's voice in the soul and in his word. This, this will go with us, to stamp itself on our future frames, to darken our future being, to separate us, like an impassable gulf, from our Creator, and from pure and happy beings, to be as a consuming fire and an undying worm.

—♦—

THE grandeur of man's nature turns to insignificance all outward distinctions. His powers of intellect, of conscience, of love, of knowing God, of perceiving the beautiful, of acting on his own mind, on outward nature, and on his fellow-creatures, — these are glorious prerogatives. Through the vulgar error of undervaluing what is common, we are apt, indeed, to pass these by as of little worth. But as in the outward creation, so in the soul, the common is the most precious. Science and art may invent splendid modes of illuminating the apartments of the opulent; but these are all poor and worthless, compared with the common light which the sun sends into all our windows, which he pours freely, impartially over hill and valley, which kindles daily the eastern and western sky; and so the common lights of reason, and conscience, and love, are of more worth and dignity than the rare endowments which give celebrity to a few.

We ought to think much more of walking in the right path than of reaching our end. We should desire virtue more than success. If by one wrong deed we could accomplish the liberation of millions, and in no other way, we ought to feel that this good, for which, perhaps, we had prayed with an agony of desire, was denied us by God, was reserved for other times and other hands.

All truth is of a prolific nature, and has connections not immediately perceived; and it may be that what we call vain speculations may, at no distant period, link themselves with some new facts or theories, and guide a profound thinker to the most important results. The ancient mathematician, when absorbed in solitary thought, little imagined that his theorems, after the lapse of ages, were to be applied, by the mind of Newton, to the solution of the mysteries of the universe, and not only to guide the astronomer through the heavens, but the navigator through the pathless ocean.

Who can measure the power of Christian philanthropy, of enlightened goodness, pouring itself forth, in prayers and persuasions, from the press and pulpit, from the lips and hearts of devoted men, and more and more binding together all the wise and good in the cause of their race? All other powers may fail. This must triumph. It is leagued with God's omnipotence. It is God himself acting in the hearts of his children. It has an ally in every conscience, in every human breast, in the wrong-doer himself.

All sincere partakers of Christian virtue are essentially one. In the spirit which pervades them dwells a uniting power found in no other tie. Though separated by oceans, they have sympathies strong and indissoluble. Accordingly, the clear, strong utterance of one gifted, inspired Christian flies through the earth. It touches kindred chords in another hemisphere. The word of such a man as Fenelon, for instance, finds its way into the souls of scattered millions. Are not he and they of one church? I thrill with joy at the name of holy men who lived ages ago. Ages do not divide us. I venerate them more for their antiquity. Are we not one body? Is not this union something real? It is not men's coming together in one building which makes a church. Suppose that, in a place of worship, I sit so near a fellow-creature as to touch him; but that there is no common feeling between us; that the truth which moves me he inwardly smiles at as a dream of fancy; that the disinterestedness which I honor he calls weakness or wild enthusiasm. How far apart are we, though visibly so near! We belong to different worlds. How much nearer am I to some pure, generous spirit in another continent, whose word has penetrated my heart, whose virtues have kindled me to emulation, whose pure thoughts are passing through my mind while I sit in the house of prayer! With which of these two have I church union?

MEN'S reasonings on practical subjects are not cold, logical processes, standing separate in the mind, but are carried on in intimate connection with their prevalent feelings and modes of thought. Generally speaking, that, and that only, is truth to a man which accords with the common tone of his mind, with the mass of his impressions, with the results of his experience, with his measure of intellectual development, and especially with those deep convictions and biases which constitute what we call character.

The exaltation of talent, as it is called, above virtue and religion, is the curse of the age.

Every man is a volume, if you know how to read him.

One of the great evils of society is, that men occupied perpetually with petty details, want general truths, want broad and fixed principles. Hence many, not wicked, are unstable, habitually inconsistent, as if they were overgrown children, rather than men.

NOTHING has so stripped Christianity of its power, as the conversion of it into a state machine, as the polluting touch of the politician, who has caused it to be preached to the lower ranks, and to be professed by the higher, in order that the old polity, with its inveterate abuses, may stand fast, and that the accumulation of property in a few hands may be undisturbed. Religion, taught for such ends, is among the worst foes of social progress.

THERE is a strong tendency in men to attach the idea of necessity to an unchanging regularity of operation, and to imagine bounds to a being who keeps one undeviating path, or who repeats himself perpetually. Hence I rejoice in miracles. They show and assert the supremacy of mind in the universe. They manifest a spiritual power which is in no degree inthralled by the laws of matter. I rejoice in these witnesses to so great a truth. I rejoice in whatever proves that this order of nature, which so often weighs on me as a chain, and which contains no promise of my perfection, is not supreme and immutable, and that the Creator is not restricted to the narrow modes of operation with which I am most familiar.

Our great and most difficult duty, as social beings, is, to derive constant aid from society without taking its yoke; to open our minds to the thoughts, reasonings, and persuasions of others, and yet to hold fast the sacred right of private judgment; to receive impulses from our fellow-beings, and yet to act from our own souls; to sympathize with others, and yet to determine our own feelings;

to act with others, and yet to follow our own consciences; to unite social deference and self-dominion; to join moral self-subsistence with social dependence; to respect others without losing self-respect; to love our friends, and to reverence our superiors, whilst our supreme homage is given to that moral perfection which no friend and no superior has realized, and which, if faithfully pursued, will often demand separation from all around us. Such is our great work as social beings, and, to perform it, we should look habitually to Jesus Christ, who was distinguished by nothing more than by moral independence, than by resisting and overcoming the world.

It is a fact worthy of serious thought, and full of solemn instruction, that many of the worst errors have grown out of the religious tendencies of the mind. So necessary is it to keep watch over our whole nature, to subject the highest sentiments to the calm, conscientious reason.

ABSOLUTE power was not meant for man. There is, indeed, an exception to this rule. There is one case in which God puts a human being, wholly defenceless, into another's hands. I refer to the child, who is wholly subjected to a parent's will. But observe how carefully, I might almost say anxiously, God has provided against the abuse of this power. He has raised up for the child, in the heart of the parent, a guardian, whom the mightiest on earth cannot resist. He has fitted the parent for this trust, by teaching him to love his offspring better than himself. No eloquence on earth is so subduing as the moaning of the infant when in pain. No reward is sweeter than that infant's smile. We say, God has put the infant in the parent's hands. Might we not more truly say, that he has put the parent into the child's power? That little being sends forth his father to toil, and makes the mother watch over him by day, and fix on him her sleepless eyes by night. No tyrant lays such a yoke. Thus God has fenced and secured from abuse the power of the parent; and yet even the parent has been known, in a moment of passion, to be cruel to his child. Is man, then, to be trusted with power over a fellow-creature, who, instead of being commended by nature to his tenderest love, belongs to a despised race, is regarded as property, is made the passive instrument of his gratification and gain? I ask no documents to prove the abuses of this power, nor do I care what is said to disprove them. Millions may rise up and tell me that the slave suffers little from cruelty. I know too much of human nature, human history, human passion, to believe them. I acquit slaveholders of all peculiar depravity. I judge them by myself. I say, that absolute power always corrupts human nature more or less. I say, that extraordinary, almost miraculous self-control is necessary to secure the slaveholder from provocation and passion; and is self-control the virtue which, above all others, grows up amidst the possession of irresponsible dominion?

PANTHEISM, if it leave man a free agent, is a comparatively harmless speculation; as we see in the case of Milton. The denial of moral freedom, could it really be believed, would prove the most fatal of errors. If Edwards's work on the will could really answer its end; if it could thoroughly persuade men that they are bound by an irresistible necessity; that their actions were fixed links in the chain of destiny; that there was but one agent, — God, — in the universe; it would be one of the most pernicious books ever issued from our press.

Happily, it is a demonstration which no man believes, which the whole consciousness contradicts.

One of the tremendous evils of the world is the monstrous accumulation of power in a few hands. Half a dozen men may, at this moment, light the fires of war through the world, may convulse all civilized nations, sweep earth and sea with armed hosts, spread desolation through the fields and bankruptcy through cities, and make themselves felt by some form of suffering through every household in Christendom.

There is one grand, all-comprehending church; and if I am a Christian, I belong to it, and no man can shut me out of it. You may exclude me from your Roman church, your Episcopal church, and your Calvinistic church, on account of supposed defects in my creed or my sect; and I am content to be excluded. But I will not be severed from the great body of Christ. Who shall sunder me from such men as Fenelon, and Pascal, and Borromeo, from Archbishop Leighton, Jeremy Taylor, and John Howard? Who can rupture the spiritual bond between these men and myself? Do I not hold them dear? Does not their spirit, flowing out through their writings and lives, penetrate my soul? Are they not a portion of my being? Am I not a different man from what I should have been, had not these and other like spirits acted on mine? And is it in the power of synod, or conclave, or of all the ecclesiastical combinations on earth, to part me from them? I am bound to them by thought and affection; and can these be suppressed by the bull of a pope, or the excommunication of a council? The soul breaks scornfully these barriers, these webs of spiders, and joins itself to the great and good; and, if it possesses their spirit, will the great and good, living or dead, cast it off because it has not enrolled itself in this or another sect? A pure mind is free of the universe. It belongs to the church, the family of the pure, in all worlds. Virtue is no local thing. It is not honorable because born in this community or that, but for its own independent and everlasting beauty. This is the bond of the universal church. No man can be excommunicated from it but by himself, by the death of goodness in his own breast. All sentences of exclusion are vain, if he do not dissolve the tie of purity which binds him to all holy souls.

Great effort from great motives is the best definition of a happy life.

Better for a minister to preach in barns or the open air, where he may speak the truth from the fulness of his soul, than to lift up in cathedrals, amidst pomp and wealth, a voice which is not true to his inward thoughts.

It is the direct influence of Trinitarianism to materialize men's conceptions of God. This system is a relapse into the error of the earliest and rudest ages, into the worship of a corporeal God. Its leading feature is, the doctrine of a God clothed with a body, and acting and speaking through a material frame, of the Infinite Divinity dying on a cross; a doctrine, which in earthliness reminds us of the mythology of the rudest pagans, and which a pious Jew, in the twilight of the Mosaic religion, would have shrunk from with horror.

He who possesses the divine powers of the soul is a great being, be his place what it may. You may clothe him with rags, may immure him in a dungeon, may chain him to slavish tasks; but he is still great. You may shut him out of your houses; but God opens to him heavenly mansions. He makes no show, indeed, in the streets of a splendid city; but a clear thought, a pure affection, a resolute act of a virtuous will, have a dignity of quite another kind, and far higher than accumulations of brick, and granite, and plaster, and stucco, however cunningly put together, or though stretching far beyond our sight.

It is a solemn duty to speak plainly of wrongs which good men perpetrate. It is very easy to cry out against crimes which the laws punish, and which popular opinion has branded with infamy. What is especially demanded of the Christian is, a faithful, honest, generous testimony against enormities which are sanctioned by numbers, and fashion, and wealth, and especially by great and honored names, and which, thus sustained, lift up their heads to heaven, and repay rebuke with menace and indignation.

THE habit of exaggerating the wretchedness of man's condition, for the purpose of rendering Jesus more necessary, operates very seriously to degrade men's love to Jesus, by accustoming them to ascribe to him a low and common-place character. Were you to see millions and millions of the human race on the edge of a fiery gulf, where ages after ages of torture awaited them, and were the shrieks of millions who had already been plunged into the abyss to pierce your ear, could you refrain from an overpowering compassion, and would you not willingly endure hours and days of exquisite pain to give these wretched millions release? Is there any man who has not virtue enough for this? I have known men of ordinary character hazard their lives under the impulse of compassion, for the rescue of fellow-beings from infinitely lighter evils than are here supposed. To me it seems, that to paint the misery of human beings in these colors of fire and blood, and to ascribe to Christ the compassion which such misery must awaken, and to make this the chief attribute of his mind, is the very method to take from his character its greatness, and to weaken his claim on our love.

Political action in this country does little to lift up any who are concerned in it. It stands in opposition to a high morality. Politics, indeed, regarded as the study and pursuit of the true, enduring good of a community, as the application of great and unchangeable principles to public affairs, is a noble sphere of thought and action; but politics, in its common sense, or considered as the invention of temporary shifts, as the playing of a subtile game, as the tactics of party for gaining power and the spoils of office, and for elevating one set of men above another, is a paltry and debasing concern.

POLITICS, however they make the intellect active, sagacious, and inventive, within a certain sphere, generally extinguish its thirst for universal truth, paralyze sentiment and imagination, corrupt the simplicity of the mind, destroy that confidence in human virtue which lies at the foundation of philanthropy and generous sacrifices, and end in cold and prudent selfishness.

IT is an interesting and solemn reflection, that the very nobleness of human nature may become the means and instrument of degradation. The powers which ally us to God, when pressed into the service of desire and appetite, enlarge desire into monstrous excess, and irritate appetite into fury. The rapidity of thought, the richness of imagination, the resources of invention, when enslaved to any passion, give it an extent and energy unknown to inferior natures; and just in the proportion that this usurper establishes its empire over us, all the nobler attainments and products of the soul perish.

It does not offend me that the Romanist maintains that a piece of bread, a wafer, over which a priest has pronounced some magical words, is the flesh and blood of Jesus Christ. I learn, indeed, in this error, an humbling lesson of human credulity, of the weakness of human reason; but I see nothing in it which strikes at the essential principles of religion. When, however, the Roman Catholic goes farther, and tells me that God looks with abhorrence on all who will not see in the consecrated wafer Christ's flesh and blood, and when he makes the reception of this from the hands of a consecrated priest the door into Christ's fold, then I am shocked by the dishonor he casts on God and virtue, by his debasing conceptions of our moral nature, and of the divine, and by his cruel disruption of the ties of human and Christian brotherhood. How sad and strange that a man educated under Christianity should place religion in a church connection, in church rites, should shut from God's family the wisest and the best, because they conscientiously abstain from certain outward ordinances! Is not holiness of heart and life dear to God for its own sake, dear to him without the manipulations of a priest, without the agency of a consecrated wafer? The grand error of Roman Catholicism is, its narrow church spirit, its blind sectarianism, its exclusion of virtuous, pious men from God's favor because they cannot eat, drink, or pray according to certain prescribed rites. Romanism has to learn that nothing but the inward life is great and good in the sight of the Omniscient, and that all who cherish this are members of Christ's body. Romanism is any thing but what it boasts to be, the universal church. I am too much a catholic to enlist under its banner.

Government resembles the wall which surrounds our lands; a needful protection, but rearing no harvests, ripening no fruits. It is the individual who must choose whether the enclosure shall be a paradise or a waste. How little positive good can government confer! It does not till our fields, build our houses, weave the ties which bind us to our families, give disinterestedness to the heart, or energy to the intellect and will. All our great interests are left to ourselves; and governments, when they have interfered with them, have obstructed, much more than advanced them. For example, they have taken religion into their keeping only to disfigure it. So education, in their hands, has become a propagator of servile maxims, and an upholder of antiquated errors. In like manner, they have paralyzed trade by their nursing care, and multiplied poverty by their expedients for its relief. Government has almost always been a barrier against which intellect has had to struggle; and society has made its chief progress by the minds of private individuals, who have outstripped their rulers, and gradually shamed them into truth and wisdom.

WHEN I compare the clamorous preaching and passionate declamation, too common in the Christian world, with the composed dignity, the deliberate wisdom, the freedom from all extravagance, which characterized Jesus, I can imagine no greater contrast; and I am sure that the fiery zealot is no representative of Christianity.

I AM persuaded that controversies about Christ's person have in one way done great injury. They have turned attention from his character. Suppose that, as Americans, we should employ ourselves in debating the questions, where Washington was born, and from what spot he came when he appeared at the head of our armies; and that, in the fervor of these contentions, we should overlook the character of his mind, the spirit that moved within him, the virtues which distinguished him, the beamings of a noble, magnanimous soul, — how unprofitably should we be employed! Who is it that understands

Washington? Is it he that can settle his rank in the creation, his early history, his present condition? or he to whom the soul of that great man is laid open, who comprehends and sympathizes with his generous purposes, who understands the energy with which he espoused the cause of freedom and his country, and who receives through admiration a portion of the same divine energy? So, in regard to Jesus, the questions which have been agitated about his rank and nature are of inferior moment. His greatness belonged not to his condition, but to his mind, his spirit, his aim, his disinterestedness, his calm, sublime consecration of himself to the high purpose of God.

The moment a man parts with moral independence; the moment he judges of duty, not from the inward voice, but from the interests and will of a party; the moment he commits himself to a leader or a body, and winks at evil, because division would hurt the cause; the moment he shakes off his particular responsibility, because he is but one of a thousand or million by whom the evil is done, — that moment he parts with his moral power. He is shorn of the energy of single-hearted faith in the right and the true. He hopes from man's policy what nothing but loyalty to God can accomplish. He substitutes coarse weapons, forged by man's wisdom, for celestial power.

He who rears up one child in Christian virtue, or recovers one fellow-creature to God, builds a temple more precious than Solomon's or St. Peter's, more enduring than earth or heaven.

It is common for those who argue against intemperance to describe the bloated countenance of the drunkard, now flushed and now deadly pale. They describe his trembling, palsied limbs. They describe his waning prosperity, his poverty, his despair. They describe his desolate, cheerless home, his cold hearth, his scanty board, his heart-broken wife, the squalidness of his children; and we groan in spirit over so sad a recital. But it is right that all this should be. It is right that he who, forewarned, puts out the lights of understanding and conscience within him, who abandons his rank among God's rational creatures, and takes his place among brutes, should stand a monument of wrath among his fellows, should be a teacher wherever he is seen — a teacher, in every look and motion, of the awful guilt of destroying reason. Were we so constituted that reason could be extinguished, and the countenance retain its freshness, the form its grace, the body its vigor, the outward condition its prosperity, and no striking change be seen in one's home, — so far from being gainers, we should lose some testimonies of God's parental care.

I CANNOT now, as I once did, talk lightly, thoughtlessly, of fighting with this or that nation. That nation is no longer an abstraction to me. It is no longer a vague mass. It spreads out before me into individuals, in a thousand interesting forms and relations. It consists of husbands and wives, parents and children, who love one another as I love my own home. It consists of affectionate women and sweet children. It consists of Christians united with me to the common Savior, and in whose spirit I recognize the likeness of his divine virtue. It consists of a vast multitude of laborers at the plough and in the workshop, whose toils I sympathize with, whose burden I should rejoice to lighten, and for whose elevation I have pleaded. It consists of men of science, taste, genius, whose writings have beguiled my solitary hours, and given life to my intellect and best affections. Here is the nation which I am called to fight with, into whose families I must send mourning, whose fall or humiliation I must seek through blood. I cannot do it without a clear commission from God.

We are immediately struck with this peculiarity in the Author of Christianity, that, while all other men are formed in a measure by the spirit of the age, we can discover in Jesus no impression of the period in which he lived. We know, with considerable accuracy, the state of society, the modes of thinking, the hopes and expectations of the country in which Jesus was born and grew up; and he is as free from them, and as exalted above them, as if he had lived in another world, or with every sense shut on the objects around him. His character has nothing in it that is local or temporary. It can be explained by nothing around him. His history shows him to us a solitary being, living for purposes which none but himself comprehended, and enjoying not so much as the sympathy of a single mind. His apostles, his chosen companions, brought to him the spirit of the age; and nothing shows its strength more strikingly, than the slowness with which it yielded, in these honest men, to the instructions of Jesus

---

A MAN in tne common walks of life, who has faith in perfection, in the unfolding of the human spirit, as the great purpose of God, possesses more the secret of the universe, perceives more the harmonies or mutual adaptations of the world without and thc world within him, is a wiser interpreter of Providence, and reads nobler lessons of duty in the events which pass before him, than the profoundest philosopher who wants this grand central truth.

THE individual is not made for the state, so much as the state for the individual. A man is not created for political relations as his highest end, but for indefinite spiritual progress, and is placed in political relations as the means of his progress. The human soul is greater, more sacred, than the state, and must never be sacrificed to it.

NEVER, never do violence to your rational nature. He who in any case admits doctrines which contradict reason, has broken down the great barrier between truth and falsehood, and lays open his mind to every delusion. The great mark of error, which is inconsistency, ceases to shock him. He has violated the first law of the intellect, and must pay the fearful penalty. Happy will it be for him, if, by the renunciation of reason, he be not prepared for the opposite extreme, and do not, through a natural reaction, rush into the excess of incredulity In the records of individuals, and of the race, it is not uncommon for an era of intellectual prostration to be followed by an era of proud and licentious philosophy; nor will this alternation cease to form this history of the human mind till the just rights of reason be revered.

Is it not to be desired that all our churches should have services to teach us our union with Christ's whole body? Would not this break our sectarian chains, and awaken reverence for Christ's spirit, for true goodness, under every name and form? It is not enough to feel that we are members of this or that narrow communion. Christianity is universal sympathy and love. I do not recommend that our churches should be lined with pictures of saints. This usage must come in, if it come at all, not by recommendation, but by gradual change of tastes and feelings. But why may not the pulpit be used occasionally to give us the lives and virtues of eminent disciples in former ages? It is customary to deliver sermons on the history of Peter, John, Paul, and of Abraham, and Elijah, and other worthies of the Old Testament; and this we do because their names are written in the Bible. But goodness owes nothing to the circumstance of its being recorded in a sacred book, nor loses its claim to grateful, reverent commemoration because not blazoned there. Moral greatness did not die out with the apostles. Their lives were reported for this, among other ends, that their virtues might be propagated to future times, and that men might spring up as worthy a place among the canonized as themselves. What I wish is, that we should learn to regard ourselves as members of a vast spiritual community, as joint heirs and fellow-worshippers with the goodly company of Christian heroes who have gone before us, instead of immuring ourselves in particular churches. Our nature delights in this consciousness of vast connection. This tendency manifests itself in the patriotic sentiment, and in the passionate clinging of men to a great religious denomination. Its true and noblest gratification is found in the deep feeling of a vital, everlasting connection with the universal church, with the innumerable multitude of the holy on earth and in heaven.

It is possible that the distance of heaven lies wholly in the veil of flesh, which we now want power to penetrate. A new sense, a new eye, might show the spiritual world compassing us on every side.

I HAVE no fears from infidelity; especially from that form of it which some are at this moment laboring to spread through our community; I mean that insane, desperate unbelief, which strives to quench the light of nature as well as of revelation, and to leave us not only without Christ, but without God. This I dread no more than I should fear the efforts of men to pluck the sun from his sphere, or to storm the skies with the artillery of the earth. We were made for religion; and unless the enemies of our faith can change our nature, they will leave the foundation of religion unshaken. The human soul was made to look above material nature. It wants a Deity for its love and trust, an immortality for its hope. It wants consolations not found in philosophy; wants strength in temptation, sorrow, and death, which human wisdom cannot minister; and knowing as I do, that Christianity meets these deep wants of men, I have no fear or doubt as to its triumphs.

THIS country has the best materials for an army in a righteous cause, and the worst in a wicked one.

WE hear much desponding language about society. The cant of the day is the cant of indifference or despair. But let it not discourage us. It is, indeed, possible that this country may sink beneath the work imposed on it by Providence, and, instead of bringing the world into its debt, may throw new darkness over human hope. But great ideas, once brought to light, do not die. The multitude of men through the civilized world are catching some glimpses, however indistinct, of a higher lot; are waking up to something higher than animal good. There is springing up an aspiration among them, which, however dreaded as a dangerous restlessness, is the natural working of the human spirit, whenever it emerges from gross ignorance, and seizes on some vague idea of its rights. Thank God, it is natural for man to aspire; and this aspiration ceases to be dangerous just in proportion as the intelligent members of society interpret it aright, and respond to it, and give themselves to the work of raising their brethren. If, through self-indulgence or pride, they decline this work, the aspiration will not cease; but growing up under resistance or contempt, it may become a spirit of hostility, conflict, revenge.

It is the tendency of increasing civilization, refinement, and expansion of mind, to produce a tone of thought and feeling unfriendly to the church spirit, to reliance on church forms as essential to salvation. As the world advances, it leaves matters of form behind. In proportion as men get into the heart of things, they are less anxious about exteriors. In proportion as religion becomes a clear reality, we grow tired of shows. In the progress of ages there spring up in greater numbers men, of mature thought and spiritual freedom, who unite self-reverence with reverence of God, and who cannot, without a feeling approaching shame and conscious degradation, submit to a church which accumulates outward, rigid, mechanical observances towards the infinite Father. A voice within them, which they cannot silence, protests against the perpetual repetition of the same signs, motions, words, as unworthy of their own spiritual powers, and of Him who deserves the highest homage of the reason and the heart. Their filial spirit protests against it. In common life, a refined, lofty mind expresses itself in simple, natural, unconstrained manners; and the same tendency, though often obstructed, is manifested in religion. The progress of Christianity, which must go on, is but another name for the growing knowledge and experience of that spiritual worship of the Father which Christ proclaimed as the end of his mission; and before this the old idolatrous reliance on ecclesiastical forms and organizations cannot stand. There is thus a perpetually swelling current which exclusive churches have to stem, and which must sooner or later sweep away their proud pretensions. What avails it that this or another church summons to its aid fathers, traditions, venerated usages? The spirit, the genius of Christianity, is stronger than all these. The great ideas of the religion must prevail over narrow, perverse interpretations of it. On this ground, I have no alarms at reports of the triumphs of the Catholic church. The spirit of Christianity is stronger than popes and councils.

If I am to be hedged in on every side, to be fretted by the perpetual presence of arbitrary will, to be denied the exercise of my powers, it matters nothing to me whether the chain is laid on me by one or many, by king or people. A despot is not more tolerable for his many heads.

When one idea predominates strongly above all others, it is a key to a nation's history. The great idea of Rome, that which the child drank in with his mother's milk, was Dominion. The great idea of France is Glory. In despotisms, the idea of the king or the church possesses itself of the minds of the people, and a superstitious loyalty or piety becomes the badge of the inhabitants. The most interesting view of this country is the grandeur of the idea which has determined its history, and which is expressed in all its institutions. Take away this, and we have nothing to distinguish us. In the refined arts, in manners, in works of genius, we are as yet surpassed. From our youth and insulated position, our history has no dazzling brilliancy. But one distinction belongs to us. A great idea, from the beginning, has been working in the minds of this people, and it broke forth with peculiar energy in our revolution. This is the idea of human rights.

SINCE the introduction of our religion, human nature has made great progress, and society experienced great changes; and in this advanced condition of the world, Christianity, instead of losing its application and importance, is found to be more and more congenial and adapted to man's nature and wants. Men have outgrown the other institutions of that period when Christianity appeared; its philosophy, its modes of warfare, its policy, its public and private economy; but Christianity has never shrunk as intellect has opened, but has always kept in advance of men's faculties, and unfolded nobler views in proportion as they have ascended. The highest powers and affections which our nature has developed, find more than adequate objects in this religion. Christianity is indeed peculiarly fitted to the more improved stages of society, to the more delicate sensibilities of refined minds, and especially to that dissatisfaction with the present state, which always grows with the growth of our moral powers and affections. As men advance in civilization, they become susceptible of mental sufferings, to which ruder ages are strangers; and these Christianity is fitted to assuage. Imagination and intellect become more restless; and Christianity brings them tranquillity, by the eternal and magnificent truths, the solemn and unbounded prospects, which it unfolds. This fitness of our religion to more advanced stages of society than that in which it was introduced, to wants of human nature not then developed, seems to me very striking. The religion bears the marks of having come from a being who perfectly understood the human mind, and had power to provide for its progress. This feature of Christianity is of the nature of prophecy. It was an anticipation of future and distant ages; and when we consider among whom our religion sprung, where, but in God, can we find an explanation of this peculiarity?

The increasing connection between a minister and the community, while it liberalizes the mind, and counteracts professional prejudices, has a tendency to enslave him to opinion, to wear away the energy of virtuous resolution, and to change him from an intrepid guardian of virtue and foe of sin, into a merely elegant and amiable companion.

We have read of certain sects, which have denounced, indiscriminately, all sports and relaxations; because these, if allowed, will be carried to excess; and of others, which have prescribed by laws the plainest, coarsest dress, because ornament, if in any measure tolerated, would certainly grow up into extravagance and vanity. And is this degrading legislation never to end? Are men never to be trusted to themselves? Is it God's method to hem them in with precise prescriptions? Does Providence leave nothing to individual discretion? Does Providence withhold every privilege which may be abused? Does Christianity enjoin an exact, unvarying round of services, because reason and conscience, if allowed to judge of duty, will often be misguided by partiality and passion? How liberal, generous, confiding, are nature, Providence, and Christianity, in their dealings with men! And when will men learn to exercise towards one another the same liberal and confiding spirit?

The Sunday which has come down to us from our fathers, seems to me exceedingly defective. The clergy have naturally taken it very much into their own hands, and I apprehend that as yet they have not discovered all the means of making it a blessing to mankind.

It is not the highest attainment to be benevolent to those who are thousands of miles from us, whose miseries make striking pictures for the imagination, who never cross our paths, never interfere with our interests, never try us by their waywardness, never shock us by their coarse manners, and whom we are to assist by an act of bounty which sends a missionary to their aid.

WE cannot be happy beyond our love.

RELIGION, if it be true, is central truth; and all knowledge which is not gathered round it, and quickened and illuminated by it, is hardly worthy the name.

WERE there a country on earth uniting all that is beautiful in nature, all that is great in virtue, genius, and the liberal arts, and numbering among its citizens the most illustrious patriots, poets, philosophers, philanthropists of our age, how eagerly should we cross the ocean to visit it! And how immeasurably greater is the attraction of heaven! There live the elder brethren of the creation, the sons of the morning, who sang for joy at the creation of our race; there the great and good of all ages and climes; the friends, benefactors, deliverers, ornaments of their race; the patriarch, prophet, apostle, and martyr; the true heroes of public, and still more of private, life; the father, mother, husband, wife, child, who, unrecorded by man, have walked before God in the beauty of love and self-sacrificing virtue. There are all who have built up in our hearts the power of goodness and truth, the writers from whose pages we have received the inspiration of pure and lofty sentiments, the friends whose countenances have shed light through our dwellings, and peace and strength through our hearts. There they are gathered together, safe from every storm, and triumphant over every evil; and they say to us, Come and join us in our everlasting blessedness; come and bear part in our song of praise; share our adoration, friendship, progress, and works of love.

ALL works of the intellect, which have not in some measure been quickened by the spirit of religion, are doomed to perish or to lose their power; and that genius is preparing for itself a sepulchre, when it disjoins itself from the universal mind.

MAN, when viewed in separation from his Maker and his end, can be as little understood and portrayed, as a plant torn from the soil in which it grew, and cut off from communication with the clouds and sun.

I HAVE been often struck by the contrast between the use made of the cross in the pulpit, and the calm, unimpassioned manner in which the sufferings of Jesus are detailed by the evangelists. These witnesses of Christ's last moments give you, in simple language, the particulars of that scene, without one remark, one word of emotion; and, if you read the Acts and Epistles, you will not find a single instance in which the apostles strove to make a moving picture of his crucifixion. No; they honored Jesus too much, they felt too deeply the greatness of his character, to be moved, as many are, by the circumstances of his death. Reverence, admiration, sympathy with his sublime spirit, — these swallowed up, in a great measure, sympathy with his sufferings. The cross was to them the last, crowning manifestation of a celestial mind; they felt that it was endured to communicate the same mind to them and the world; and their emotion was a holy joy in this consummate and unconquerable goodness. To be touched by suffering is a light thing. It is not the greatness of Christ's sufferings on the cross which is to move our whole souls, but the greatness of the spirit with which he suffered. To approach the cross for the purpose of weeping over a bleeding, dying friend, is to lose the chief influence of the crucifixion. We are to visit the cross, not to indulge a natural softness, but to acquire firmness of spirit, to fortify our minds for hardship and suffering in the cause of duty and of human happiness.

Religion carries its own evidence with it more than history or science. It should rest more on the soul's own consciousness, experience, and observation.

We must not look round on the universe with awe, and on man with scorn; for man, who can comprehend the universe and its laws, "is greater than the universe, which cannot comprehend itself." God dwells in every human being more intimately than in the outward creation. The voice of God comes to us in the ocean, the thunder, the whirlwind, but how much more of God is there in his inward voice, in the intuitions of reason, in the rebukes of conscience, in the whispers of the Holy Spirit! I would have you see God in the awful mountain, and in the tranquil valley; but more, much more, in the clear judgment, the moral energy, the disinterested purpose, the pious gratitude, the immortal hope, of a good man.

When I compare together different classes, as existing at this moment in the civilized world, I cannot think the difference between the rich and the poor, in regard to mere physical suffering, so great as is sometimes imagined. That some of the indigent among us die of scanty food, is undoubtedly true; but vastly more, in this community, die from eating too much, than from eating too little; vastly more from excess than starvation. So, as to clothing, many shiver from want of defences against the cold; but there is vastly more suffering among the rich from absurd and criminal modes of dress, which fashion has sanctioned, than among the poor from deficiency of raiment. Our daughters are oftener brought to the grave by their rich attire, than our beggars by their nakedness. So the poor are often overworked; but they suffer less than many among the rich, who have no work to do, no interesting object to fill up life, to satisfy the infinite cravings of man for action. According to our present modes of education, how many of our daughters are victims of *ennui!* — a misery unknown to the poor, and more intolerable than the weariness of excessive toil. The idle young man, spending the day in exhibiting his person in the street, ought not to excite the envy of the overtasked poor; and this cumberer of the ground is found exclusively among the rich.

CRIMES exalted into laws become therefore the more odious; just as the false gods of heathenism, when set up of old on the altar of Jehovah, shocked his true worshippers the more by usurping so conspicuously the honors due to him alone.

THE south is fond of calling itself Anglo-Saxon. Judging from character, I should say this name belongs much more to the north, the country of steady, persevering, unconquerable energy. Our southern brethren remind me more of the Normans. They seem to have in their veins the burning blood of that pirate race, who spread terror through

Europe, who seized part of France as a prey, and then pounced on England; a conquering, chivalrous race, from which most of the noble families of England are said to be derived.

All noble enthusiasms pass through a feverish stage, and grow wiser and more serene.

The saddest aspect of the age, to me, is that which undoubtedly contributes to social order. It is the absorption of the multitude of men in outward, material interests; it is the selfish prudence which is never tired of the labor of accumulation, and which keeps men steady, regular, respectable drudges, from morning to night. The cases of a few murders, great crimes, lead multitudes to exclaim, How wicked this age! But the worst sign is the chaining down of almost all the minds of a community to low, perishable interests. It is a sad thought, that the infinite energies of the soul have no higher end than to cover the back, and fill the belly, and keep caste in society. A few nerves, hardly visible, on the surface of the tongue, create most of the endless stir around us. Undoubtedly, eating and drinking, dressing, house-building, and caste-keeping, are matters not to be despised; most of them are essential. But surely life has a higher use than to adorn this body, which is so soon to be wrapped in grave-clothes; than to keep warm and flowing the blood, which is so soon to be cold and stagnant in the tomb. I rejoice in the boundless activity of the age, and I expect much of it to be given to our outward wants. But over all this activity there should preside the great idea of that which is alone ourselves; of our inward, spiritual nature; of the thinking, immortal soul; of our supreme good, our chief end, which is, to bring out, cultivate, and perfect our highest powers; to become wise, holy, disinterested, noble beings; to unite ourselves to God by love and adoration, and to revere his image in his children

---

The doctrine of the Trinity seems to me only fitted to throw a mistiness over Christ, to place him beyond the reach of our understanding and hearts. When I am told that Jesus Christ is the second person in the Trinity, one of three persons who constitute one God, one infinite mind, I am plunged into an abyss of darkness. Jesus becomes to me the most unintelligible being in the universe. God I can know. Man I can understand. But Christ, as described in human creeds, a compound being, at once man and God, at once infinite in wisdom, and ignorant of innumerable truths, and who is so united with two other persons as to make with them one mind, —

Christ so represented baffles all my faculties. I cannot lay hold on him. My weak intellect is wholly at fault. This is a grave objection to the doctrine of the Trinity. It destroys the reality, the distinctness, the touching nearness of Jesus Christ. It gives him an air of fiction, and has done more than all things to prevent a true, deep acquaintance with him, with his spirit, with the workings of his mind, with the sublimity of his virtue. It has thrown a glare over him, under which the bright and beautiful features of his character have been very much concealed.

WHERE, but from God himself, can I learn my destination? I ask at the mouth of the tomb for intelligence of the departed, and the tomb gives me no reply. I examine the various regions of nature, but I can discover no process for restoring the mouldering body, and no sign or track of the spirit's ascent to another sphere. I see the need of a power above nature to restore or perpetuate life after death; and if God intended to give assurance of this life, I see not how he can do it but by supernatural teaching, by a miraculous revelation. Miracles are the appropriate, and would seem to be the only, mode of placing beyond doubt man's future and immortal being; and no miracles can be conceived so peculiarly adapted to this end as the very ones which hold the highest place in Christianity. I mean the resurrection of Lazarus, and, still more, the resurrection of Jesus.

I HONOR the passion for power and rule as little in the people as in a king. It is a vicious principle, exist where it may. If by democracy be meant the exercise of sovereignty by the people under all those provisions and self-imposed restraints which tend most to secure equal laws, and the rights of each and all, then I shall be proud to bear its name. But the unfettered multitude is not dearer to me than the unfettered king.

MEN will prefer even a fanaticism which is in earnest, to a pretended rationality, which leaves untouched all the great springs of the soul, which never lays a quickening hand on our love and veneration, our awe and fear, our hope and joy.

THE spirit of society, not an outward institution, is the mighty power by which the hard lot of man is to be meliorated.

THE fate of this country depends on nothing so much as on the growth or decline of the great idea which lies at the foundation of all our institutions — the idea of the sacredness of every man's right, the respect due to every human being. This exists among us. It has stamped itself on government. It is now to stamp itself on manners and common life — a far harder work. It will then create a society such as men have not anticipated, but which is not to be despaired of, if Christianity be divine, or if the highest aspirations of the soul be true.

You tell me of civilization, of its arts and sciences, as the sure instruments of human elevation. You tell me how by these man masters and bends to his use the powers of nature. I know he masters them, but it is in turn to become their slave. He explores and cultivates the earth, but it is to grow more earthly. He explores the hidden mine, but it is to forge himself chains. He visits all regions, but therefore lives a stranger to his own soul. In the very progress of civilization, I see the need of an antagonist principle to the senses, of a power to free man from matter, to recall him from the outward to the inward world; and religion alone is equal to so great a work.

NOTHING would be more unjust than to decide on men's characters from their peculiarities of faith; and the reason is plain. Such peculiarities are not the only causes which impress and determine the mind. Our nature is exposed to innumerable other influences. If, indeed, a man were to know nothing but his creed; were to meet no human beings but those who adopt it; were to see no example, and to hear no conversation, but such as were formed by it; if his creed were to meet him every where, and to exclude every other object of thought,—then his character might be expected to answer to it with great precision. But our Creator has not shut us up in so narrow a school. The mind is exposed to an infinite variety of influences, and these are multiplying with the progress of society. Education, friendship, neighborhood, public opinion, the state of society, "the genius of the place" where we live, books, events, the pleasures and business of life, the outward creation, our physical temperament, and innumerable other causes, are perpetually pouring in upon the soul thoughts, views, and emotions; and these influences are so complicated, so peculiarly combined in the case of every individual, and so modified by the original susceptibilities and constitution of every mind, that on no subject is there greater uncertainty, than on the formation of character. To determine the precise operation of a religious opinion amidst this host of influences, surpasses human power. A great truth may be completely neutralized by the countless impressions and excitements which the mind received from other sources; and so a great error may be disarmed of much of its power by the superior energy of other and better views, of early habits, and of virtuous examples. Nothing is more common than to see a doctrine believed without swaying the will. Its efficacy depends not on the assent of the intellect, but on the place which it occupies in the thoughts, on the distinctness and vividness with which it is conceived, on its associations with our common ideas, on its frequency of recurrence, and on its command of the attention, without which it has no life. Accordingly, pernicious opinions are not seldom held by men of the most illustrious virtue. I mean not, then, in commending or condemning systems, to pass sentence on their professors. I know the power of the mind to select from a multifarious system, for its habitual use, those features or principles which are generous, pure, and ennobling, and by these to sustain its spiritual life amidst the nominal profession of many errors. I know that a creed is one thing, as written in a book, and another, as it exists in the minds of its advocates. In the book, all the doctrines appear in equally strong and legible lines. In the mind, many are faintly traced, and seldom recurred to, whilst others are inscribed as with sunbeams, and are the chosen, constant lights of the soul. Hence, in good men of opposing denominations, a real agreement may subsist as to their vital principles of faith; and amidst the division of tongues, there may be unity of soul, and the same internal worship of God.

THE very religion given to exalt human nature, has been used to make it abject. The very religion which was given to create a generous hope, has been made an instrument of servile and torturing fear. The very religion which came from God's goodness to enlarge the soul with a kindred goodness, has been employed to narrow it to a sect, to rear the Inquisition, and to kindle fires for the martyr. The very religion given to make the understanding and conscience free, has, by a criminal perversion, served to break them into a subjection to priests, ministers, and human creeds. Ambition and craft have seized on the solemn doctrines of an omnipotent God and of future punishment, and turned them into engines against the child, the trembling female, the ignorant adult, until the skeptic has been imboldened to charge on religion the chief miseries and degradation of human nature.

WHEN I place side by side the mighty works of Jesus and the prodigies of heathenism, I see that they can no more be compared with one another, than the machinery and mock thunders of the theatre can be likened to the awful and beneficent powers of the universe.

THE Romish church is illustrated by great names. Her gloomy convents have often been brightened by fervent love to God and man. Her St. Louis, and Fenelon, and Massillon, and Cheverus; her missionaries, who have carried Christianity to the ends of the earth; her Sisters of Charity, who have carried relief and solace to the most hopeless want and pain, — do not these teach us that in the Romish church the Spirit of God has found a home? How much, too, have other churches to boast! In the English church we meet the names of Latimer, Hooker, Barrow, Leighton, Berkeley, and Heber; in the dissenting Calvinistic church, Baxter, Howe, Watts, Doddridge, and Robert Hall; among the Quakers, George Fox, William Penn,

Robert Barclay, and our own Anthony Benezet and John Woolman; in the anti-Trinitarian church, John Milton, John Locke, Samuel Clarke, Price, and Priestley. To repeat these names does the heart good. They breathe a fragrance through the common air. They lift up the whole race to which they belong. With the churches of which they were pillars or chief ornaments I have many sympathies; nor do I condemn the union of ourselves to these or any other churches whose doctrines we approve, provided that we do it without severing ourselves in the least from the universal church. On this point we cannot be too earnest. We must shun the spirit of sectarianism as from hell. We must shudder at the thought of shutting up God in any denomination. We must think no man the better for belonging to our communion; no man the worse for belonging to another. We must look with undiminished joy on goodness, though it shine forth from the most adverse sect. Christ's spirit must be equally dear and honored, no matter where manifested. To confine God's love or his good spirit to any party, sect, or name, is to sin against the fundamental law of the kingdom of God, to break that living bond with Christ's universal church which is one of our chief helps to perfection.

Royalty is impotence and a vulgar show, compared with the deep and quickening power which many a Christian teacher has exerted on the immortal soul.

Man was made for relaxation as truly as for labor; and by a law of his nature, which has not received the attention it deserves, he finds, perhaps, no relaxation so restorative, as that in which he reverts to his childhood, seems to forget his wisdom, leaves the imagination to exhilarate itself by sportive inventions, talks of amusing incongruities in conduct and events, smiles at the innocent eccentricities and odd mistakes of those whom he most esteems, allows himself in arch allusions or kind-hearted satire, and transports himself into a world of ludicrous combinations. We have said, that, on these occasions, the mind seems to put off its wisdom; but the truth is, that, in a pure mind, wisdom retreats, if we may so say, to its centre, and there, unseen, keeps guard over this transient folly, draws delicate lines which are never to be passed in the freest moments, and, like a judicious parent watching the sports of childhood, preserves a stainless innocence of soul in the very exuberance of gayety.

We think the decline of Calvinism one of the most encouraging facts in our passing history; for this system, by outraging conscience and reason, tends to array these high faculties against revelation.

GREAT thoughts and great emotions have a place in human history which no historian has hitherto given them; and the future is to be more determined by these than the past.

THE doctrine of an infinite atonement is wholly delusion. The Trinitarian tells me that, according to his system, we have an infinite substitute; that the infinite God was pleased to bear our punishment, and, consequently, that pardon is made sure. But I ask him, Do I understand you? Do you mean that the great God, who never changes, whose happiness is the same yesterday, to-day, and forever, — that this eternal being really bore the penalty of my sins, really suffered and died? Every pious man, when pressed by this question, answers, No. What, then, does the doctrine of infinite atonement mean? Why, this; that God took into union with himself our nature, that is, a human body and soul; and these bore the sufferings for our sins; and, through his union with these, God may be said to have borne it himself. Thus this vaunted system goes out, — in words. The infinite victim proves to be frail man, and God's share in the sacrifice is a mere fiction. I ask with solemnity, Can this doctrine give one moment's ease to the conscience of an unbiased, thinking man? Does it not unsettle all hope, by making the whole religion suspicious and unsure? I am compelled to say that I see in it no impression of majesty, or wisdom, or love, nothing worthy of a God; and when I compare it with that nobler faith which directs our eyes and hearts to God's essential mercy, as our only hope, I am amazed that any should ascribe to it superior efficacy, as a religion for sinners, as a means of filling the soul with a pious trust and love.

I CANNOT but pity the man who recognizes nothing godlike in his own nature. I see the marks of God in the heaven and the earth, but how much more in a liberal intellect, in magnanimity, in unconquerable rectitude, in a philanthropy which forgives every wrong, and which never despairs of the cause of Christ and human virtue! I do, and I must, reverence human nature. Neither the sneers of a worldly skepticism, nor the groans of a gloomy theology, disturb my faith in its godlike powers and tendencies. I know how it is despised, how it has been oppressed, how civil and religious establishments have for ages conspired to crush it. I know its history. I shut my eyes on none of its weaknesses and crimes. I understand the proofs by which despotism demonstrates that man is a wild beast, in want of a master, and only safe in chains. But, injured, trampled on, and scorned, as our nature is, I still turn to it with intense sympathy and strong hope. The signatures of its origin and its end are impressed too deeply to be ever wholly effaced. I bless it for its kind affections, for its strong and tender love. I honor it for its struggles against oppression, for its growth and progress under the weight of so many chains and prejudices, for its achievements in science and art, and still more for its examples of heroic and saintly virtue. These are marks of a divine origin, and the pledges of a celestial inheritance; and I thank God that my own lot is bound up with that of the human race.

Without religion, we can hardly escape self-contempt, and the contempt of our race. Without God, our existence has no support, our life no aim, our improvements no permanence, our best labors no sure and enduring results, our spiritual weakness no power to lean upon, and our noblest aspirations and desires no pledge of being realized in a better state. Struggling virtue has no friend, suffering virtue no promise of victory. Take away God, and life becomes mean, and man poorer than the brute.

When I think what Christianity has become in the hands of politicians and priests; how it has been shaped into a weapon of power; how it has crushed the human soul for ages; how it has struck the intellect with palsy, and haunted the imagination with superstitious phantoms; how it has broken whole nations to the yoke, and frowned on every free thought; — when I think how, under almost every form of this religion, its ministers have taken it into their own keeping, have hewn and compressed it into the shape of rigid creeds, and have then pursued by menaces of everlasting woe whosoever should question the divinity of these works of their hands; when I consider, in a word, how, under such influences, Christianity has been, and still is, exhibited in forms which shock alike the reason, conscience, and heart, — I feel deeply, painfully, what a different system it is from that which Jesus taught, and I dare not apply to unbelief the terms of condemnation which belonged to the infidelity of the primitive age.

It is a false idea that religion requires the extermination of any principle, desire, appetite, or passion, which our Creator has implanted. Our nature is a whole, a beautiful whole, and no part can be spared. You might as properly and innocently lop off a limb from the body, as eradicate any natural desire from the mind. All our appetites are in themselves innocent and useful, ministering to the general weal of the soul. They are like the elements of the natural world, parts of a wise and beneficent system, but, like those elements, are beneficent only when restrained.

The worst abuses of our religion have sprung from a cowardly want of confidence in its power. Its friends have feared that it could not stand without a variety of artificial buttresses. They have imagined that men must now be bribed into faith by annexing to it temporal privileges, now driven into it by menaces and inquisitions, now attracted by gorgeous forms, now awed by mysteries and superstitions; in a word, that the multitude must be imposed upon, or the religion will fall. I have no such distrust of Christianity; I believe in its invincible powers. It is founded in our nature. It meets our deepest wants. Its proofs, as well as principles, are adapted to the common understandings of men, and need not to be aided by appeals to fear, or any other passion, which would discourage inquiry or disturb the judgment. I fear nothing for Christianity, if left to speak in its own tones, to approach men with its unveiled, benignant countenance. I do fear much from the weapons of policy and intimidation, which are framed to uphold the imagined weakness of Christian truth.

When I see a man holding faster his uprightness in proportion as it is assailed; fortifying his religious trust in proportion as Providence is obscure; hoping in the ultimate triumphs of virtue more surely in proportion to its present afflictions; cherishing philanthropy amidst the discouraging experience of men's unkindness and unthankfulness; extending to others a sympathy which his own sufferings need, but cannot obtain; growing milder and gentler amidst what tends to exasperate and harden; and, through inward principle, converting the very incitements to evil into the occasions of a victorious virtue, — I see an explanation, and a noble explanation, of the present state. I see a good produced, so transcendent in its nature as to justify all the evil and suffering under which it grows up. I should think the formation of a few such minds worth all the apparatus of the present world. I should say that this earth, with its continents and oceans, its seasons and harvests, and its successive generations, was a work worthy of God, even were it to accomplish no other end than the training and manifestation of the illustrious characters which are scattered through history. And when I consider how small a portion of human virtue is recorded by history, how superior in dignity, as well as in number, are the unnoticed, unhonored saints and heroes of domestic and humble life, I see a light thrown over the present state which more than reconciles me to all its evils.

There is no end to the volumes written in defence of this or that church which sets itself forth as the only true church, and claims exclusive acceptance with God. But the unlettered Christian has an answer to them all. He cannot, and need not, seek it in libraries. He finds it, almost without seeking, in plain passages of the New Testament, and in his own heart. He reads, and he feels, that religion is an inward life. This he knows, not by report, but by consciousness, by the prostration of his soul in penitence, by the surrender of his will to the Divine, by overflowing gratitude, by calm trust, and by a new love to his fellow-creatures. Will it do to tell such a man that the promises of Christianity do not belong to him, that access to God is denied him, because he is not joined with this or that exclusive church? Has not this access been granted to him already? Has he not prayed in his griefs, and been consoled? in his temptations, and been strengthened? Has he not found God near in his solitudes and in the great congregation? Does he thirst for any thing so fervently as for perfect assimilation to the divine purity? And can he question God's readiness to help him, because he is unable to find in Scripture a command to bind himself to this or another self-magnifying church? How easily does the experience of true Christians brush away the cobwebs of theologians! He loves and reveres God, and in this spirit has a foretaste of heaven; and can heaven be barred against him by ecclesiastical censures? He has felt the power of the cross, and resurrection, and promises of Jesus Christ; and is there any "height or depth" of human exclusiveness and bigotry which can separate him from his Lord? He can die for truth and humanity; and is there any man so swelled by the conceit of his union with the true church as to stand apart, and say, "I am holier than thou"?

It is a remarkable fact, that the very spirit to which Christianity is most hostile, the passion for power, dominion, pomp, and preëminence, struck its deepest roots in the church. The church became the very stronghold of the lusts and vices which Christianity most abhors. Accordingly, its history is one of the most melancholy records of past times.

Error soon passes away, unless upheld by restraint on thought. History tells us, — and the lesson is invaluable, — that the physical force which has put down free inquiry has been the main bulwark of the superstitions and illusions of past ages.

FACTS are often placed beyond doubt by the effects which they leave behind them. This is the case with the miracles of Christ. Let me explain this branch of evidence. I am told, when absent and distant from your city, that, on a certain day, a tide, such as had never been known, rose in your harbor, overflowed your wharves, and rushed into your streets. I doubt the fact. But hastening here, I see what were once streets strowed with sea-weed, and shells, and the ruins of houses, and I cease to doubt. A witness may deceive, but such effects cannot lie. All great events leave effects, and these speak directly of the cause. What, I ask, are the proofs of the American revolution? Have we none but written or oral testimony?

Our free constitution, the whole form of our society, the language and spirit of our laws, — all these bear witness to our English origin, and to our successful conflict for independence. Now, the miracles of Christianity have left effects, which equally attest their reality, and cannot be explained without them. I go back to the age of Jesus Christ, and I am immediately struck with the commencement and rapid progress of the most remarkable revolution in the annals of the world. I see a new religion, of a character altogether its own, which bore no likeness to any past or existing faith, spreading, in a few years, through all civilized nations, and introducing a new era, a new state of society, a change of the human mind, which has broadly distinguished all following ages. Here is a plain fact, which the skeptic will not deny, however he may explain it. I see this religion issuing from an obscure, despised, hated people. Its Founder had died on the cross — a mode of punishment as disgraceful as the pillory or gallows of the present day. Its teachers were poor men, without rank, office, or education, taken from the fishing-boat and other occupations which had never furnished teachers to mankind. I see these men beginning their work on the spot where their Master's blood had been shed, as of a common malefactor; and I hear them summoning first his murderers, and then all nations and all ranks, the sovereign on the throne, the priest in the temple, the great and the learned, as well as the poor and the ignorant, to renounce the faith and the worship which had been hallowed by the veneration of all ages, and to take the yoke of their crucified Lord. I see passion and prejudice, the sword of the magistrate, the curse of the priest, the scorn of the philosopher, and the fury of the populace, joined to crush this common enemy; and yet, without a human weapon, and in opposition to all human power, I see the humble apostles of Jesus winning their way, overpowering prejudice, breaking the ranks of their opposers, changing enemies into friends, breathing into multitudes a calm spirit of martyrdom, and carrying to the bounds of civilization, and even into half-civilized regions, a religion which has contributed to advance society more than all other causes combined. Here is the effect. Here is a monument more durable than pillars or triumphal arches. Now, I ask for an explanation of these effects. If Jesus Christ and his apostles were indeed sent and empowered by God, and wrought miracles in attestation of their mission, then the establishment of Christianity is explained. Suppose them, on the other hand, to have been insane enthusiasts, or selfish impostors, left to meet the whole strength of human opposition, with nothing but their own power, or rather their own weakness, and you have no cause for the stupendous effect I have described. Such men could no more have changed the face of the world, than they could have turned back rivers to their sources, sunk mountains into valleys, or raised valleys to the skies. Christianity, then, has not only the evidence of unexceptionable witnesses, but that of effects — a proof which will grow stronger by comparing its progress with that of other religions, such as Mahometanism, which sprung from human passions, and were advanced by human power.

It is a privilege to have lived in an age so stirring, so pregnant, so eventful. It is an age never to be forgotten. Its voice of warning and encouragement is never to die. Its impression on history is indelible. Amidst its events, the American revolution, the first distinct, solemn assertion of the rights of men, and the French revolution, that volcanic force which shook the earth to its centre, are never to pass from men's minds. Over this age the night will indeed gather more and more as time rolls away; but in that night two forms will appear, — Washington and Napoleon, — the one a lurid meteor, the other a benign, serene, and undecaying star.

HUMAN nature is not a tiger which needs a constant chain. In this case, it is the chain which makes the tiger. It is the oppressor who has made man fit only for a yoke.

THE ministers who deal most in terrors, who preach doctrines which ought to make their flesh creep, and to turn their eyes into fountains of tears, are not generally distinguished by their spare forms and haggard countenances. They take the world as easily as people of a milder creed; and this does not show that they want sincerity or benevolence. It only shows how superficially men may believe in doctrines which yet they would shudder to relinquish. It shows how little the import of language, which is thundered from the lips, is comprehended and felt. I should not set down as hard-hearted a man whose appetite should be improved by preaching a sermon full of images and threatenings of "a bottomless hell." The best meals are sometimes made after such effusions. This is only an example of the numberless contradictions of human life. Men are every day saying and doing, from the power of education, habit, and imitation, what has no root whatever in their serious convictions.

Other religions have been intended to meet the exigencies of particular countries or times, and therefore society, in its progress, has outgrown them; but

Christianity meets more and more the wants of the soul in proportion to the advancement of our race, and thus proves itself to be Eternal Truth.

In the long run, truth is aided by nothing so much as by opposition, and by the opposition of those who can give the full strength of the argument on the side of error.

When I think of the vast capacities of the human mind, of God's nearness to it and unbounded love towards it, I am disposed to wonder, not that revelations have been made, but that they have not been more variously vouchsafed to the wants of mankind.

It is one distinction of modern over ancient times, that we have grown more patient of toil. Our danger is from habits of drudgery. The citizens of Greece and Rome were above work. We seem to work with something of the instinct of the ant and the bee.

The glory of an age is often hidden from itself. Perhaps some word has been spoken in our day which we have not deigned to hear, but which is to grow clearer and louder through all ages. Perhaps some silent thinker among us is at work in his closet, whose name is to fill the earth. Perhaps there sleeps in his cradle some reformer, who is to move the church and the world, who is to open a new era in history, who is to fire the human soul with new hope and new daring.

There is one consolation attending persecution. It often exalts the spirit of the sufferer, and often covers with honor those whom it had destined to shame. Who made Socrates the most venerable name of antiquity? The men who mixed for him the cup of hemlock, and drove him as a criminal from the world which he had enlightened. Providence teaches us the doctrine of retribution very touchingly in the fact, that future ages guard with peculiar reverence the memories of men, who, in their own times, were contemned, abhorred, hunted like wild beasts, and destroyed by fire or sword, for their fidelity to truth.

When I set before me true virtue, all the distinctions on which men value themselves fade away. Wealth is poor; worldly honor is mean; outward forms are beggarly elements. Condition, country, church, all sink into unimportance. Before this simple greatness I bow, I revere. The robed priest, the gorgeous altar, the great assembly, the pealing organ, all the exteriors of religion, vanish from my sight as I look at the good and great man, the holy, disinterested soul. Even I, with vision so dim, with heart so cold, can see and feel the divinity, the grandeur of true goodness. How, then, must God regard it? To his pure eye how lovely must it be! And can any of us turn from it, because some water has not been dropped on its forehead, or some bread put into its lips by a minister or priest? or because it has not learned to repeat some mysterious creed, which a church or human council has ordained?

It is a problem in history, how the English people, so sturdy and stout-hearted in the main, could be so tame and flexible, in matters of religion, under Henry the Eighth, Edward the Sixth, Mary, and Elizabeth. They seem to have received, almost as unresistingly as the coin, the image and superscription of the king. The causes of this yieldingness are to be found in the averseness to civil broils to which the nation had been brought by the recent bloody and exhausting wars of the Roses; in the formidable power of the Tudor sovereigns; in the insular position of England, and her distance from Rome, which checked the domination of the Papacy; in the ignorance of the people; in the ravenousness of the nobles for the property of the church in the first instance, and afterwards in their greediness for court favor. This strange pliancy is a stain on the annals of the country. It was in the Puritans that the old national sturdiness revived, that England became herself again. These men were rude in aspect and forbidding in manners; but, with all their sternness, narrowness, frowning theology, and high religious pretensions, they were the master spirits of their times. To their descendants it is delightful to think of the service they rendered to the civil and religious liberties of England and the world, and to recall their deep, vital piety — a gem most rudely set, but too precious to be overvalued.

THE inventions of printing, of gunpowder, and the mariner's compass, were too mean affairs for History to trace. She was bowing before kings and warriors. She had volumes for the plots and quarrels of Leicester and Essex in the reign of Elizabeth, but not a page for Shakspeare; and if Bacon had not filled an office, she would hardly have recorded his name, in her anxiety to preserve the deeds and sayings of that Solomon of his age, James the First.

WHEN I trace the unaffected majesty which runs through the life of Jesus, and see him never falling below his sublime claims, amidst poverty, and scorn, and in his last agony, I have a feeling of the reality of his character which I cannot express. I feel that the Jewish carpenter could no more have conceived and sustained this character under motives of imposture, than an infant's arm could repeat the deeds of Hercules, or his unawakened intellect comprehend and rival the matchless works of genius.

THE END.

www.ingramcontent.com/pod-product-compliance
Lightning Source LLC
LaVergne TN
LVHW021405110826
845150LV00007B/1787

* 9 7 8 1 4 2 5 5 1 2 6 0 6 *